Journal

BY:

Natalie Watson

Copyright © 2021

ISBN: 978-1-9991021-2-8

When we think of grieving, we automatically associate it with death and the loss of our loved ones that is dearest to our hearts. We can grief in many ways, such as the loss of a friend that ended unexpectedly, the loss of a successful career, or the loss of ones feeling of belonging.

What is the definition of grief?

noun

"Deep sorrow, especially that is caused by someone's **death**"

This book is for everyone, we will all be confronted with the loss of someone or something in this lifetime.

I have learned and understand that there are four types of grief.

- ⚘ **Bereavement** - The death of a loved one.
- ⚘ **Loss** - When a treasure or extremely important possession is taken away.
- ⚘ **Acute** - Emotional, physical and behavioural.
- ⚘ **Complicated** - Uncontrollable feelings and obsessive thoughts.

I have also learned that there are five stages of grief.

- **Denial**
- **Anger**
- **Bargaining**
- **Depression**
- **Acceptance**

Each role of the five stages of grieving plays an important role in your healing process and does not go in any order. One can start with anger before moving to denial and depression. Sometimes we are unaware where we may end up on the list, its important to stop and take a breath allowing the roller coaster of energy find its way out. I am not here to tell you how to grief; however, I have experienced the loss of my son and I know what it is exactly what you are experiencing.

I will keep it 100% with you. When I first heard the news that my son passed away on May 29th, 2018, I thought life ended for me that instant. I wanted an outlet to document my thoughts, emotions and all that was going through my mind. Let us just say it felt as though I was on a roller coaster flying off its track. I documented all those emotions on a plain line paper where I journaled my experience daily, which turned into writing my 1st book, "Fifteen Years And 14 Chapters", The Loss of My Son in Three ways".

Now thinking back to that day; I can recall thinking to myself, I wished there were a little bit more colour and excitement to my journal. I wanted a journal that could have assisted me with my overall process of healing. I craved for ways on how I can express myself starting from inside and working on my outward. The feeling of becoming whole and having some sort of normalcy in my life again was as important to me just as the air that I breath.

Ask yourself these questions and think of it as part of your healing and where you are today.

- Are there things in your life that you are still grieving?
- How has it affected you?
- Can you picture yourself a month or 6 months from now?

I Definitely could not have processed even on a day-to-day basis, how was I going to live another day after experiencing the loss of my son the third time. I had no clarity, no pathway, and to make matters worst I struggled with even forming a sentence without biting the tip of my tongue.

Writing out your thoughts on paper can help you in several ways.

- Opening your mind to imagine all the possibilities around healing.
- Writing out your thoughts promotes a healthy way of healing.
- Clarity relaxes the tension in your mind, body and soul.
- Understanding and working through grief is the best gift you can give to yourself.
- Documenting your journey keeps you in control of your life and happiness.
- Reflecting on the process creates extra room for growth.
- Most importantly, understanding that grieving is a fundamental part of your mental health and well being.

Embrace each and everyday as it comes and always remember the journey of healing starts with you. May this process assist you on your journey of a lifetime of healing, grieving the loss of a friendship, the loss of your loved ones, or the loss of something that was extremely important and dear to you heart. You can document and express your thoughts and feelings here daily. Trust your process and take care of yourself on this journey.

Dedicated to Noah Matthew Watson

Today I am grieving the loss of

_____

_____

_____

What was the date of your loss?

_____

_____

_____

Express the grief you feel in 10 words

_____

_____

_____

List 10 things worth striving for

_____

_____

_____

"I am still healing, and the journey of healing starts with me"

DAY 1

Today I am grieving the loss of

_____

_____

_____

What was the date of your loss?

_____

_____

_____

Express the grief you feel in 10 words

_____

_____

_____

List 10 things worth striving for

_____

_____

_____

"I am still healing, and the journey of healing starts with me"

Today I am grieving the loss of

_____

_____

_____

What was the date of your loss?

_____

_____

_____

Express the grief you feel in 10 words

_____

_____

_____

List 10 things worth striving for

_____

_____

_____

"I am still healing, and the journey of healing starts with me"

Today I am grieving the loss of

_____
_____
_____

What was the date of your loss?

_____
_____
_____

Express the grief you feel in 10 words

_____
_____
_____

List 10 things worth striving for

_____
_____
_____

"I am still healing, and the journey of healing starts with me"

DAY 4

Today I am grieving the loss of

_____

_____

_____

What was the date of your loss?

_____

_____

_____

Express the grief you feel in 10 words

_____

_____

_____

List 10 things worth striving for

_____

_____

_____

"I am still healing, and the journey of healing starts with me"

Today I am grieving the loss of

_____

_____

_____

What was the date of your loss?

_____

_____

_____

Express the grief you feel in 10 words

_____

_____

_____

List 10 things worth striving for

_____

_____

_____

"I am still healing, and the journey of healing starts with me"

Today I am grieving the loss of

_____
_____
_____

What was the date of your loss?

_____
_____
_____

Express the grief you feel in 10 words

_____
_____
_____

List 10 things worth striving for

_____
_____
_____

"I am still healing, and the journey of healing starts with me"

DAY 7

Today I am grieving the loss of

_____

_____

_____

What was the date of your loss?

_____

_____

_____

Express the grief you feel in 10 words

_____

_____

_____

List 10 things worth striving for

_____

_____

_____

"I am still healing, and the journey of healing starts with me"

Today I am grieving the loss of

_____

_____

_____

What was the date of your loss?

_____

_____

_____

Express the grief you feel in 10 words

_____

_____

_____

List 10 things worth striving for

_____

_____

_____

"I am still healing, and the journey of healing starts with me"

Today I am grieving the loss of

_____

_____

_____

What was the date of your loss?

_____

_____

_____

Express the grief you feel in 10 words

_____

_____

_____

List 10 things worth striving for

_____

_____

_____

"I am still healing, and the journey of healing starts with me"

DAY 10

Today I am grieving the loss of

_____

_____

_____

What was the date of your loss?

_____

_____

_____

Express the grief you feel in 10 words

_____

_____

_____

List 10 things worth striving for

_____

_____

_____

"I am still healing, and the journey of healing starts with me"

Today I am grieving the loss of

_____

_____

_____

What was the date of your loss?

_____

_____

_____

Express the grief you feel in 10 words

_____

_____

_____

List 10 things worth striving for

_____

_____

_____

"I am still healing, and the journey of healing starts with me"

DAY 12

Today I am grieving the loss of

___

What was the date of your loss?

___

Express the grief you feel in 10 words

___

List 10 things worth striving for

___

"I am still healing, and the journey of healing starts with me"

DAY 13

Today I am grieving the loss of

_____

_____

_____

What was the date of your loss?

_____

_____

_____

Express the grief you feel in 10 words

_____

_____

_____

List 10 things worth striving for

_____

_____

_____

"I am still healing, and the journey of healing starts with me"

Today I am grieving the loss of

_____
_____
_____

What was the date of your loss?

_____
_____
_____

Express the grief you feel in 10 words

_____
_____
_____

List 10 things worth striving for

_____
_____
_____

"I am still healing, and the journey of healing starts with me"

DAY 15

Today I am grieving the loss of

_____

_____

_____

What was the date of your loss?

_____

_____

_____

Express the grief you feel in 10 words

_____

_____

_____

List 10 things worth striving for

_____

_____

_____

"I am still healing, and the journey of healing starts with me"

DAY 16

Today I am grieving the loss of

_____

_____

_____

What was the date of your loss?

_____

_____

_____

Express the grief you feel in 10 words

_____

_____

_____

List 10 things worth striving for

_____

_____

_____

"I am still healing, and the journey of healing starts with me"

DAY 17

Today I am grieving the loss of

_____
_____
_____

What was the date of your loss?

_____
_____
_____

Express the grief you feel in 10 words

_____
_____
_____

List 10 things worth striving for

_____
_____
_____

"I am still healing, and the journey of healing starts with me"

DAY 18

Today I am grieving the loss of

_____
_____
_____

What was the date of your loss?

_____
_____
_____

Express the grief you feel in 10 words

_____
_____
_____

List 10 things worth striving for

_____
_____
_____

"I am still healing, and the journey of healing starts with me"

DAY 19

Today I am grieving the loss of

_____

_____

_____

What was the date of your loss?

_____

_____

_____

Express the grief you feel in 10 words

_____

_____

_____

List 10 things worth striving for

_____

_____

_____

"I am still healing, and the journey of healing starts with me"

DAY 20

Today I am grieving the loss of

_____

_____

_____

What was the date of your loss?

_____

_____

_____

Express the grief you feel in 10 words

_____

_____

_____

List 10 things worth striving for

_____

_____

_____

"I am still healing, and the journey of healing starts with me"

DAY 21

Today I am grieving the loss of

_____

_____

_____

What was the date of your loss?

_____

_____

_____

Express the grief you feel in 10 words

_____

_____

_____

List 10 things worth striving for

_____

_____

_____

"I am still healing, and the journey of healing starts with me"

DAY 22

Today I am grieving the loss of

___

What was the date of your loss?

___

Express the grief you feel in 10 words

___

List 10 things worth striving for

___

"I am still healing, and the journey of healing starts with me"

DAY 23

Today I am grieving the loss of

_____

_____

_____

What was the date of your loss?

_____

_____

_____

Express the grief you feel in 10 words

_____

_____

_____

List 10 things worth striving for

_____

_____

_____

"I am still healing, and the journey of healing starts with me"

DAY 24

Today I am grieving the loss of

_____

_____

_____

What was the date of your loss?

_____

_____

_____

Express the grief you feel in 10 words

_____

_____

_____

List 10 things worth striving for

_____

_____

_____

"I am still healing, and the journey of healing starts with me"

DAY 25

Today I am grieving the loss of

_____

_____

_____

What was the date of your loss?

_____

_____

_____

Express the grief you feel in 10 words

_____

_____

_____

List 10 things worth striving for

_____

_____

_____

"I am still healing, and the journey of healing starts with me"

Today I am grieving the loss of

_____

_____

_____

What was the date of your loss?

_____

_____

_____

Express the grief you feel in 10 words

_____

_____

_____

List 10 things worth striving for

_____

_____

_____

"I am still healing, and the journey of healing starts with me"

DAY 27

Today I am grieving the loss of

_____

_____

_____

What was the date of your loss?

_____

_____

_____

Express the grief you feel in 10 words

_____

_____

_____

List 10 things worth striving for

_____

_____

_____

"I am still healing, and the journey of healing starts with me"

Today I am grieving the loss of

_____

_____

_____

What was the date of your loss?

_____

_____

_____

Express the grief you feel in 10 words

_____

_____

_____

List 10 things worth striving for

_____

_____

_____

"I am still healing, and the journey of healing starts with me"

DAY 29

Today I am grieving the loss of

_____

_____

_____

What was the date of your loss?

_____

_____

_____

Express the grief you feel in 10 words

_____

_____

_____

List 10 things worth striving for

_____

_____

_____

"I am still healing, and the journey of healing starts with me"

DAY 30

Today I am grieving the loss of

_____
_____
_____

What was the date of your loss?

_____
_____
_____

Express the grief you feel in 10 words

_____
_____
_____

List 10 things worth striving for

_____
_____
_____

"I am still healing, and the journey of healing starts with me"

DAY 31

Today I am grieving the loss of

_____

_____

_____

What was the date of your loss?

_____

_____

_____

Express the grief you feel in 10 words

_____

_____

_____

List 10 things worth striving for

_____

_____

_____

"I am still healing, and the journey of healing starts with me"

Today I am grieving the loss of

_____

_____

_____

What was the date of your loss?

_____

_____

_____

Express the grief you feel in 10 words

_____

_____

_____

List 10 things worth striving for

_____

_____

_____

"I am still healing, and the journey of healing starts with me"

DAY 33

Today I am grieving the loss of

___

What was the date of your loss?

___

Express the grief you feel in 10 words

___

List 10 things worth striving for

___

"I am still healing, and the journey of healing starts with me"

DAY 34

Today I am grieving the loss of

_____
_____
_____

What was the date of your loss?

_____
_____
_____

Express the grief you feel in 10 words

_____
_____
_____

List 10 things worth striving for

_____
_____
_____

"I am still healing, and the journey of healing starts with me"

Today I am grieving the loss of

_____

_____

_____

What was the date of your loss?

_____

_____

_____

Express the grief you feel in 10 words

_____

_____

_____

List 10 things worth striving for

_____

_____

_____

"I am still healing, and the journey of healing starts with me"

DAY 36

Today I am grieving the loss of

What was the date of your loss?

Express the grief you feel in 10 words

List 10 things worth striving for

"I am still healing, and the journey of healing starts with me"

Today I am grieving the loss of

_____

_____

_____

What was the date of your loss?

_____

_____

_____

Express the grief you feel in 10 words

_____

_____

_____

List 10 things worth striving for

_____

_____

_____

"I am still healing, and the journey of healing starts with me"

DAY 38

Today I am grieving the loss of

___

What was the date of your loss?

___

Express the grief you feel in 10 words

___

List 10 things worth striving for

___

"I am still healing, and the journey of healing starts with me"

Today I am grieving the loss of

_____

_____

_____

What was the date of your loss?

_____

_____

_____

Express the grief you feel in 10 words

_____

_____

_____

List 10 things worth striving for

_____

_____

_____

"I am still healing, and the journey of healing starts with me"

DAY 40

Today I am grieving the loss of

_____

_____

_____

What was the date of your loss?

_____

_____

_____

Express the grief you feel in 10 words

_____

_____

_____

List 10 things worth striving for

_____

_____

_____

"I am still healing, and the journey of healing starts with me"

DAY 41

Today I am grieving the loss of

_____

_____

_____

What was the date of your loss?

_____

_____

_____

Express the grief you feel in 10 words

_____

_____

_____

List 10 things worth striving for

_____

_____

_____

"I am still healing, and the journey of healing starts with me"

Today I am grieving the loss of

_____

_____

_____

What was the date of your loss?

_____

_____

_____

Express the grief you feel in 10 words

_____

_____

_____

List 10 things worth striving for

_____

_____

_____

"I am still healing, and the journey of healing starts with me"

Today I am grieving the loss of

_____

_____

_____

What was the date of your loss?

_____

_____

_____

Express the grief you feel in 10 words

_____

_____

_____

List 10 things worth striving for

_____

_____

_____

"I am still healing, and the journey of healing starts with me"

Today I am grieving the loss of

_____

_____

_____

What was the date of your loss?

_____

_____

_____

Express the grief you feel in 10 words

_____

_____

_____

List 10 things worth striving for

_____

_____

_____

"I am still healing, and the journey of healing starts with me"

Today I am grieving the loss of

_____

_____

_____

What was the date of your loss?

_____

_____

_____

Express the grief you feel in 10 words

_____

_____

_____

List 10 things worth striving for

_____

_____

_____

"I am still healing, and the journey of healing starts with me"

Today I am grieving the loss of

_____

_____

_____

What was the date of your loss?

_____

_____

_____

Express the grief you feel in 10 words

_____

_____

_____

List 10 things worth striving for

_____

_____

_____

"I am still healing, and the journey of healing starts with me"

Today I am grieving the loss of

_____

_____

_____

What was the date of your loss?

_____

_____

_____

Express the grief you feel in 10 words

_____

_____

_____

List 10 things worth striving for

_____

_____

_____

"I am still healing, and the journey of healing starts with me"

DAY 48

Today I am grieving the loss of

_____
_____
_____

What was the date of your loss?

_____
_____
_____

Express the grief you feel in 10 words

_____
_____
_____

List 10 things worth striving for

_____
_____
_____

"I am still healing, and the journey of healing starts with me"

DAY 49

Today I am grieving the loss of

_____

_____

_____

What was the date of your loss?

_____

_____

_____

Express the grief you feel in 10 words

_____

_____

_____

List 10 things worth striving for

_____

_____

_____

"I am still healing, and the journey of healing starts with me"

DAY 50

Today I am grieving the loss of

_____
_____
_____

What was the date of your loss?

_____
_____
_____

Express the grief you feel in 10 words

_____
_____
_____

List 10 things worth striving for

_____
_____
_____

"I am still healing, and the journey of healing starts with me"

DAY 51

Today I am grieving the loss of

_____

_____

_____

What was the date of your loss?

_____

_____

_____

Express the grief you feel in 10 words

_____

_____

_____

List 10 things worth striving for

_____

_____

_____

"I am still healing, and the journey of healing starts with me"

DAY 52

Today I am grieving the loss of

_____

_____

_____

What was the date of your loss?

_____

_____

_____

Express the grief you feel in 10 words

_____

_____

_____

List 10 things worth striving for

_____

_____

_____

"I am still healing, and the journey of healing starts with me"

Today I am grieving the loss of

___

What was the date of your loss?

___

Express the grief you feel in 10 words

___

List 10 things worth striving for

___

"I am still healing, and the journey of healing starts with me"

DAY 54

Today I am grieving the loss of

_____

_____

_____

What was the date of your loss?

_____

_____

_____

Express the grief you feel in 10 words

_____

_____

_____

List 10 things worth striving for

_____

_____

_____

"I am still healing, and the journey of healing starts with me"

DAY 55

Today I am grieving the loss of

_____

_____

_____

What was the date of your loss?

_____

_____

_____

Express the grief you feel in 10 words

_____

_____

_____

List 10 things worth striving for

_____

_____

_____

"I am still healing, and the journey of healing starts with me"

DAY 56

Today I am grieving the loss of

_____

_____

_____

What was the date of your loss?

_____

_____

_____

Express the grief you feel in 10 words

_____

_____

_____

List 10 things worth striving for

_____

_____

_____

"I am still healing, and the journey of healing starts with me"

Today I am grieving the loss of

_____

_____

_____

What was the date of your loss?

_____

_____

_____

Express the grief you feel in 10 words

_____

_____

_____

List 10 things worth striving for

_____

_____

_____

"I am still healing, and the journey of healing starts with me"

DAY 58

Today I am grieving the loss of

_____
_____
_____

What was the date of your loss?

_____
_____
_____

Express the grief you feel in 10 words

_____
_____
_____

List 10 things worth striving for

_____
_____
_____

"I am still healing, and the journey of healing starts with me"

Today I am grieving the loss of

___

What was the date of your loss?

___

Express the grief you feel in 10 words

___

List 10 things worth striving for

___

"I am still healing, and the journey of healing starts with me"

Today I am grieving the loss of

_____

_____

_____

What was the date of your loss?

_____

_____

_____

Express the grief you feel in 10 words

_____

_____

_____

List 10 things worth striving for

_____

_____

_____

"I am still healing, and the journey of healing starts with me"

Today I am grieving the loss of

_____

_____

_____

What was the date of your loss?

_____

_____

_____

Express the grief you feel in 10 words

_____

_____

_____

List 10 things worth striving for

_____

_____

_____

"I am still healing, and the journey of healing starts with me"

DAY 62

Today I am grieving the loss of

_____

_____

_____

What was the date of your loss?

_____

_____

_____

Express the grief you feel in 10 words

_____

_____

_____

List 10 things worth striving for

_____

_____

_____

"I am still healing, and the journey of healing starts with me"

DAY 63

Today I am grieving the loss of

_____

_____

_____

What was the date of your loss?

_____

_____

_____

Express the grief you feel in 10 words

_____

_____

_____

List 10 things worth striving for

_____

_____

_____

"I am still healing, and the journey of healing starts with me"

Today I am grieving the loss of

___

What was the date of your loss?

___

Express the grief you feel in 10 words

___

List 10 things worth striving for

___

"I am still healing, and the journey of healing starts with me"

Today I am grieving the loss of

_____

_____

_____

What was the date of your loss?

_____

_____

_____

Express the grief you feel in 10 words

_____

_____

_____

List 10 things worth striving for

_____

_____

_____

"I am still healing, and the journey of healing starts with me"

DAY 66

Today I am grieving the loss of

_____

_____

_____

What was the date of your loss?

_____

_____

_____

Express the grief you feel in 10 words

_____

_____

_____

List 10 things worth striving for

_____

_____

_____

"I am still healing, and the journey of healing starts with me"

Today I am grieving the loss of

_____

_____

_____

What was the date of your loss?

_____

_____

_____

Express the grief you feel in 10 words

_____

_____

_____

List 10 things worth striving for

_____

_____

_____

"I am still healing, and the journey of healing starts with me"

DAY 68

Today I am grieving the loss of

_____

_____

_____

What was the date of your loss?

_____

_____

_____

Express the grief you feel in 10 words

_____

_____

_____

List 10 things worth striving for

_____

_____

_____

"I am still healing, and the journey of healing starts with me"

Today I am grieving the loss of

_____

_____

_____

What was the date of your loss?

_____

_____

_____

Express the grief you feel in 10 words

_____

_____

_____

List 10 things worth striving for

_____

_____

_____

"I am still healing, and the journey of healing starts with me"

DAY 70

Today I am grieving the loss of

___

What was the date of your loss?

___

Express the grief you feel in 10 words

___

List 10 things worth striving for

___

"I am still healing, and the journey of healing starts with me"

Today I am grieving the loss of

_____
_____
_____

What was the date of your loss?

_____
_____
_____

Express the grief you feel in 10 words

_____
_____
_____

List 10 things worth striving for

_____
_____
_____

"I am still healing, and the journey of healing starts with me"

Today I am grieving the loss of

_____

_____

_____

What was the date of your loss?

_____

_____

_____

Express the grief you feel in 10 words

_____

_____

_____

List 10 things worth striving for

_____

_____

_____

"I am still healing, and the journey of healing starts with me"

Today I am grieving the loss of

_____

_____

_____

What was the date of your loss?

_____

_____

_____

Express the grief you feel in 10 words

_____

_____

_____

List 10 things worth striving for

_____

_____

_____

"I am still healing, and the journey of healing starts with me"

DAY 74

Today I am grieving the loss of

_____

_____

_____

What was the date of your loss?

_____

_____

_____

Express the grief you feel in 10 words

_____

_____

_____

List 10 things worth striving for

_____

_____

_____

"I am still healing, and the journey of healing starts with me"

Today I am grieving the loss of

___

___

___

What was the date of your loss?

___

___

___

Express the grief you feel in 10 words

___

___

___

List 10 things worth striving for

___

___

___

"I am still healing, and the journey of healing starts with me"

DAY 76

Today I am grieving the loss of

___

What was the date of your loss?

___

Express the grief you feel in 10 words

___

List 10 things worth striving for

___

"I am still healing, and the journey of healing starts with me"

DAY 77

Today I am grieving the loss of

_____
_____
_____

What was the date of your loss?

_____
_____
_____

Express the grief you feel in 10 words

_____
_____
_____

List 10 things worth striving for

_____
_____
_____

"I am still healing, and the journey of healing starts with me"

Today I am grieving the loss of

_____

_____

_____

What was the date of your loss?

_____

_____

_____

Express the grief you feel in 10 words

_____

_____

_____

List 10 things worth striving for

_____

_____

_____

"I am still healing, and the journey of healing starts with me"

DAY 79

Today I am grieving the loss of

_____

_____

_____

What was the date of your loss?

_____

_____

_____

Express the grief you feel in 10 words

_____

_____

_____

List 10 things worth striving for

_____

_____

_____

"I am still healing, and the journey of healing starts with me"

DAY 80

Today I am grieving the loss of

_____

_____

_____

What was the date of your loss?

_____

_____

_____

Express the grief you feel in 10 words

_____

_____

_____

List 10 things worth striving for

_____

_____

_____

"I am still healing, and the journey of healing starts with me"

Today I am grieving the loss of

_____

_____

_____

What was the date of your loss?

_____

_____

_____

Express the grief you feel in 10 words

_____

_____

_____

List 10 things worth striving for

_____

_____

_____

"I am still healing, and the journey of healing starts with me"

Today I am grieving the loss of

_____

_____

_____

What was the date of your loss?

_____

_____

_____

Express the grief you feel in 10 words

_____

_____

_____

List 10 things worth striving for

_____

_____

_____

"I am still healing, and the journey of healing starts with me"

DAY 83

Today I am grieving the loss of

___

What was the date of your loss?

___

Express the grief you feel in 10 words

___

List 10 things worth striving for

___

"I am still healing, and the journey of healing starts with me"

DAY 84

Today I am grieving the loss of

_____

_____

_____

What was the date of your loss?

_____

_____

_____

Express the grief you feel in 10 words

_____

_____

_____

List 10 things worth striving for

_____

_____

_____

"I am still healing, and the journey of healing starts with me"

Today I am grieving the loss of

_____

_____

_____

What was the date of your loss?

_____

_____

_____

Express the grief you feel in 10 words

_____

_____

_____

List 10 things worth striving for

_____

_____

_____

"I am still healing, and the journey of healing starts with me"

Today I am grieving the loss of

___

What was the date of your loss?

___

Express the grief you feel in 10 words

___

List 10 things worth striving for

___

"I am still healing, and the journey of healing starts with me"

DAY 87

Today I am grieving the loss of

_____

_____

_____

What was the date of your loss?

_____

_____

_____

Express the grief you feel in 10 words

_____

_____

_____

List 10 things worth striving for

_____

_____

_____

"I am still healing, and the journey of healing starts with me"

DAY 88

Today I am grieving the loss of

_____
_____
_____

What was the date of your loss?

_____
_____
_____

Express the grief you feel in 10 words

_____
_____
_____

List 10 things worth striving for

_____
_____
_____

"I am still healing, and the journey of healing starts with me"

Today I am grieving the loss of

___

What was the date of your loss?

___

Express the grief you feel in 10 words

___

List 10 things worth striving for

___

"I am still healing, and the journey of healing starts with me"

DAY 90

Today I am grieving the loss of

_____

_____

_____

What was the date of your loss?

_____

_____

_____

Express the grief you feel in 10 words

_____

_____

_____

List 10 things worth striving for

_____

_____

_____

"I am still healing, and the journey of healing starts with me"

Today I am grieving the loss of

_____

_____

_____

What was the date of your loss?

_____

_____

_____

Express the grief you feel in 10 words

_____

_____

_____

List 10 things worth striving for

_____

_____

_____

"I am still healing, and the journey of healing starts with me"

DAY 92

Today I am grieving the loss of

_____

_____

_____

What was the date of your loss?

_____

_____

_____

Express the grief you feel in 10 words

_____

_____

_____

List 10 things worth striving for

_____

_____

_____

"I am still healing, and the journey of healing starts with me"

Today I am grieving the loss of

_____

_____

_____

What was the date of your loss?

_____

_____

_____

Express the grief you feel in 10 words

_____

_____

_____

List 10 things worth striving for

_____

_____

_____

"I am still healing, and the journey of healing starts with me"

DAY 94

Today I am grieving the loss of

_____

_____

_____

What was the date of your loss?

_____

_____

_____

Express the grief you feel in 10 words

_____

_____

_____

List 10 things worth striving for

_____

_____

_____

"I am still healing, and the journey of healing starts with me"

Today I am grieving the loss of

_____

_____

_____

What was the date of your loss?

_____

_____

_____

Express the grief you feel in 10 words

_____

_____

_____

List 10 things worth striving for

_____

_____

_____

"I am still healing, and the journey of healing starts with me"

Today I am grieving the loss of

___

What was the date of your loss?

___

Express the grief you feel in 10 words

___

List 10 things worth striving for

___

"I am still healing, and the journey of healing starts with me"

DAY 97

Today I am grieving the loss of

_____

_____

_____

What was the date of your loss?

_____

_____

_____

Express the grief you feel in 10 words

_____

_____

_____

List 10 things worth striving for

_____

_____

_____

"I am still healing, and the journey of healing starts with me"

DAY 98

Today I am grieving the loss of

_____

_____

_____

What was the date of your loss?

_____

_____

_____

Express the grief you feel in 10 words

_____

_____

_____

List 10 things worth striving for

_____

_____

_____

"I am still healing, and the journey of healing starts with me"

Today I am grieving the loss of

_____

_____

_____

What was the date of your loss?

_____

_____

_____

Express the grief you feel in 10 words

_____

_____

_____

List 10 things worth striving for

_____

_____

_____

"I am still healing, and the journey of healing starts with me"

DAY 100

Today I am grieving the loss of

_____

_____

_____

What was the date of your loss?

_____

_____

_____

Express the grief you feel in 10 words

_____

_____

_____

List 10 things worth striving for

_____

_____

_____

"I am still healing, and the journey of healing starts with me"

DAY 101

Today I am grieving the loss of

_____

_____

_____

What was the date of your loss?

_____

_____

_____

Express the grief you feel in 10 words

_____

_____

_____

List 10 things worth striving for

_____

_____

_____

"I am still healing, and the journey of healing starts with me"

DAY 102

Today I am grieving the loss of

_____

_____

_____

What was the date of your loss?

_____

_____

_____

Express the grief you feel in 10 words

_____

_____

_____

List 10 things worth striving for

_____

_____

_____

"I am still healing, and the journey of healing starts with me"

DAY 103

Today I am grieving the loss of

_____

_____

_____

What was the date of your loss?

_____

_____

_____

Express the grief you feel in 10 words

_____

_____

_____

List 10 things worth striving for

_____

_____

_____

"I am still healing, and the journey of healing starts with me"

Today I am grieving the loss of

_____

_____

_____

What was the date of your loss?

_____

_____

_____

Express the grief you feel in 10 words

_____

_____

_____

List 10 things worth striving for

_____

_____

_____

"I am still healing, and the journey of healing starts with me"

DAY 105

Today I am grieving the loss of

_____

_____

_____

What was the date of your loss?

_____

_____

_____

Express the grief you feel in 10 words

_____

_____

_____

List 10 things worth striving for

_____

_____

_____

"I am still healing, and the journey of healing starts with me"

DAY 106

Today I am grieving the loss of

_____

_____

_____

What was the date of your loss?

_____

_____

_____

Express the grief you feel in 10 words

_____

_____

_____

List 10 things worth striving for

_____

_____

_____

"I am still healing, and the journey of healing starts with me"

Today I am grieving the loss of

_____

_____

_____

What was the date of your loss?

_____

_____

_____

Express the grief you feel in 10 words

_____

_____

_____

List 10 things worth striving for

_____

_____

_____

"I am still healing, and the journey of healing starts with me"

Today I am grieving the loss of

_____

_____

_____

What was the date of your loss?

_____

_____

_____

Express the grief you feel in 10 words

_____

_____

_____

List 10 things worth striving for

_____

_____

_____

"I am still healing, and the journey of healing starts with me"

Today I am grieving the loss of

_____

_____

_____

What was the date of your loss?

_____

_____

_____

Express the grief you feel in 10 words

_____

_____

_____

List 10 things worth striving for

_____

_____

_____

"I am still healing, and the journey of healing starts with me"

DAY 110

Today I am grieving the loss of

___

What was the date of your loss?

___

Express the grief you feel in 10 words

___

List 10 things worth striving for

___

"I am still healing, and the journey of healing starts with me"

DAY 111

Today I am grieving the loss of

___
___
___

What was the date of your loss?

___
___
___

Express the grief you feel in 10 words

___
___
___

List 10 things worth striving for

___
___
___

"I am still healing, and the journey of healing starts with me"

DAY 112

Today I am grieving the loss of

___

What was the date of your loss?

___

Express the grief you feel in 10 words

___

List 10 things worth striving for

___

"I am still healing, and the journey of healing starts with me"

DAY 113

Today I am grieving the loss of

_____

_____

_____

What was the date of your loss?

_____

_____

_____

Express the grief you feel in 10 words

_____

_____

_____

List 10 things worth striving for

_____

_____

_____

"I am still healing, and the journey of healing starts with me"

DAY 114

Today I am grieving the loss of

_____

_____

_____

What was the date of your loss?

_____

_____

_____

Express the grief you feel in 10 words

_____

_____

_____

List 10 things worth striving for

_____

_____

_____

"I am still healing, and the journey of healing starts with me"

DAY 115

Today I am grieving the loss of

___

___

___

What was the date of your loss?

___

___

___

Express the grief you feel in 10 words

___

___

___

List 10 things worth striving for

___

___

___

"I am still healing, and the journey of healing starts with me"

DAY 116

Today I am grieving the loss of

_____

_____

_____

What was the date of your loss?

_____

_____

_____

Express the grief you feel in 10 words

_____

_____

_____

List 10 things worth striving for

_____

_____

_____

"I am still healing, and the journey of healing starts with me"

DAY 117

Today I am grieving the loss of

_____

_____

_____

What was the date of your loss?

_____

_____

_____

Express the grief you feel in 10 words

_____

_____

_____

List 10 things worth striving for

_____

_____

_____

"I am still healing, and the journey of healing starts with me"

DAY 118

Today I am grieving the loss of

_____

_____

_____

What was the date of your loss?

_____

_____

_____

Express the grief you feel in 10 words

_____

_____

_____

List 10 things worth striving for

_____

_____

_____

"I am still healing, and the journey of healing starts with me"

Today I am grieving the loss of

_____
_____
_____

What was the date of your loss?

_____
_____
_____

Express the grief you feel in 10 words

_____
_____
_____

List 10 things worth striving for

_____
_____
_____

"I am still healing, and the journey of healing starts with me"

DAY 120

Today I am grieving the loss of

___

What was the date of your loss?

___

Express the grief you feel in 10 words

___

List 10 things worth striving for

___

"I am still healing, and the journey of healing starts with me"

Today I am grieving the loss of

_____

_____

_____

What was the date of your loss?

_____

_____

_____

Express the grief you feel in 10 words

_____

_____

_____

List 10 things worth striving for

_____

_____

_____

"I am still healing, and the journey of healing starts with me"

Today I am grieving the loss of

___

___

___

What was the date of your loss?

___

___

___

Express the grief you feel in 10 words

___

___

___

List 10 things worth striving for

___

___

___

"I am still healing, and the journey of healing starts with me"

DAY 123

Today I am grieving the loss of

_____
_____
_____

What was the date of your loss?

_____
_____
_____

Express the grief you feel in 10 words

_____
_____
_____

List 10 things worth striving for

_____
_____
_____

"I am still healing, and the journey of healing starts with me"

DAY 124

Today I am grieving the loss of

_____

_____

_____

What was the date of your loss?

_____

_____

_____

Express the grief you feel in 10 words

_____

_____

_____

List 10 things worth striving for

_____

_____

_____

"I am still healing, and the journey of healing starts with me"

Today I am grieving the loss of

_____

_____

_____

What was the date of your loss?

_____

_____

_____

Express the grief you feel in 10 words

_____

_____

_____

List 10 things worth striving for

_____

_____

_____

"I am still healing, and the journey of healing starts with me"

DAY 126

Today I am grieving the loss of

_____

_____

_____

What was the date of your loss?

_____

_____

_____

Express the grief you feel in 10 words

_____

_____

_____

List 10 things worth striving for

_____

_____

_____

"I am still healing, and the journey of healing starts with me"

Today I am grieving the loss of

_____
_____
_____

What was the date of your loss?

_____
_____
_____

Express the grief you feel in 10 words

_____
_____
_____

List 10 things worth striving for

_____
_____
_____

"I am still healing, and the journey of healing starts with me"

Today I am grieving the loss of

_____

_____

_____

What was the date of your loss?

_____

_____

_____

Express the grief you feel in 10 words

_____

_____

_____

List 10 things worth striving for

_____

_____

_____

"I am still healing, and the journey of healing starts with me"

Today I am grieving the loss of

_____

_____

_____

What was the date of your loss?

_____

_____

_____

Express the grief you feel in 10 words

_____

_____

_____

List 10 things worth striving for

_____

_____

_____

"I am still healing, and the journey of healing starts with me"

DAY 130

Today I am grieving the loss of

___

What was the date of your loss?

___

Express the grief you feel in 10 words

___

List 10 things worth striving for

___

"I am still healing, and the journey of healing starts with me"

Today I am grieving the loss of

_____

_____

_____

What was the date of your loss?

_____

_____

_____

Express the grief you feel in 10 words

_____

_____

_____

List 10 things worth striving for

_____

_____

_____

"I am still healing, and the journey of healing starts with me"

DAY 132

Today I am grieving the loss of

___

What was the date of your loss?

___

Express the grief you feel in 10 words

___

List 10 things worth striving for

___

"I am still healing, and the journey of healing starts with me"

DAY 133

Today I am grieving the loss of

_____

_____

_____

What was the date of your loss?

_____

_____

_____

Express the grief you feel in 10 words

_____

_____

_____

List 10 things worth striving for

_____

_____

_____

"I am still healing, and the journey of healing starts with me"

Today I am grieving the loss of

___

What was the date of your loss?

___

Express the grief you feel in 10 words

___

List 10 things worth striving for

___

"I am still healing, and the journey of healing starts with me"

DAY 135

Today I am grieving the loss of

_____

_____

_____

What was the date of your loss?

_____

_____

_____

Express the grief you feel in 10 words

_____

_____

_____

List 10 things worth striving for

_____

_____

_____

"I am still healing, and the journey of healing starts with me"

DAY 136

Today I am grieving the loss of

___

What was the date of your loss?

___

Express the grief you feel in 10 words

___

List 10 things worth striving for

___

"I am still healing, and the journey of healing starts with me"

DAY 137

Today I am grieving the loss of

_____

_____

_____

What was the date of your loss?

_____

_____

_____

Express the grief you feel in 10 words

_____

_____

_____

List 10 things worth striving for

_____

_____

_____

"I am still healing, and the journey of healing starts with me"

DAY 138

Today I am grieving the loss of

_____

_____

_____

What was the date of your loss?

_____

_____

_____

Express the grief you feel in 10 words

_____

_____

_____

List 10 things worth striving for

_____

_____

_____

"I am still healing, and the journey of healing starts with me"

DAY 139

Today I am grieving the loss of

___

What was the date of your loss?

___

Express the grief you feel in 10 words

___

List 10 things worth striving for

___

"I am still healing, and the journey of healing starts with me"

Today I am grieving the loss of

___

What was the date of your loss?

___

Express the grief you feel in 10 words

___

List 10 things worth striving for

___

"I am still healing, and the journey of healing starts with me"

DAY 141

Today I am grieving the loss of

_____

_____

_____

What was the date of your loss?

_____

_____

_____

Express the grief you feel in 10 words

_____

_____

_____

List 10 things worth striving for

_____

_____

_____

"I am still healing, and the journey of healing starts with me"

Today I am grieving the loss of

_____

_____

_____

What was the date of your loss?

_____

_____

_____

Express the grief you feel in 10 words

_____

_____

_____

List 10 things worth striving for

_____

_____

_____

"I am still healing, and the journey of healing starts with me"

DAY 143

Today I am grieving the loss of

_____

_____

_____

What was the date of your loss?

_____

_____

_____

Express the grief you feel in 10 words

_____

_____

_____

List 10 things worth striving for

_____

_____

_____

"I am still healing, and the journey of healing starts with me"

DAY 144

Today I am grieving the loss of

_____
_____
_____

What was the date of your loss?

_____
_____
_____

Express the grief you feel in 10 words

_____
_____
_____

List 10 things worth striving for

_____
_____
_____

"I am still healing, and the journey of healing starts with me"

Today I am grieving the loss of

___
___
___

What was the date of your loss?

___
___
___

Express the grief you feel in 10 words

___
___
___

List 10 things worth striving for

___
___
___

"I am still healing, and the journey of healing starts with me"

DAY 146

Today I am grieving the loss of

_____

_____

_____

What was the date of your loss?

_____

_____

_____

Express the grief you feel in 10 words

_____

_____

_____

List 10 things worth striving for

_____

_____

_____

"I am still healing, and the journey of healing starts with me"

Today I am grieving the loss of

_____
_____
_____

What was the date of your loss?

_____
_____
_____

Express the grief you feel in 10 words

_____
_____
_____

List 10 things worth striving for

_____
_____
_____

"I am still healing, and the journey of healing starts with me"

Today I am grieving the loss of

_____

_____

_____

What was the date of your loss?

_____

_____

_____

Express the grief you feel in 10 words

_____

_____

_____

List 10 things worth striving for

_____

_____

_____

"I am still healing, and the journey of healing starts with me"

DAY 149

Today I am grieving the loss of

_____

_____

_____

What was the date of your loss?

_____

_____

_____

Express the grief you feel in 10 words

_____

_____

_____

List 10 things worth striving for

_____

_____

_____

"I am still healing, and the journey of healing starts with me"

DAY 150

Today I am grieving the loss of

_____

_____

_____

What was the date of your loss?

_____

_____

_____

Express the grief you feel in 10 words

_____

_____

_____

List 10 things worth striving for

_____

_____

_____

"I am still healing, and the journey of healing starts with me"

DAY 151

Today I am grieving the loss of

_____

_____

_____

What was the date of your loss?

_____

_____

_____

Express the grief you feel in 10 words

_____

_____

_____

List 10 things worth striving for

_____

_____

_____

"I am still healing, and the journey of healing starts with me"

DAY 152

Today I am grieving the loss of

_____
_____
_____

What was the date of your loss?

_____
_____
_____

Express the grief you feel in 10 words

_____
_____
_____

List 10 things worth striving for

_____
_____
_____

"I am still healing, and the journey of healing starts with me"

Today I am grieving the loss of

_____

_____

_____

What was the date of your loss?

_____

_____

_____

Express the grief you feel in 10 words

_____

_____

_____

List 10 things worth striving for

_____

_____

_____

"I am still healing, and the journey of healing starts with me"

DAY 154

Today I am grieving the loss of

_____

_____

_____

What was the date of your loss?

_____

_____

_____

Express the grief you feel in 10 words

_____

_____

_____

List 10 things worth striving for

_____

_____

_____

"I am still healing, and the journey of healing starts with me"

DAY 155

Today I am grieving the loss of

_____

_____

_____

What was the date of your loss?

_____

_____

_____

Express the grief you feel in 10 words

_____

_____

_____

List 10 things worth striving for

_____

_____

_____

"I am still healing, and the journey of healing starts with me"

DAY 156

Today I am grieving the loss of

___

What was the date of your loss?

___

Express the grief you feel in 10 words

___

List 10 things worth striving for

___

"I am still healing, and the journey of healing starts with me"

DAY 157

Today I am grieving the loss of

___

What was the date of your loss?

___

Express the grief you feel in 10 words

___

List 10 things worth striving for

___

"I am still healing, and the journey of healing starts with me"

DAY 158

Today I am grieving the loss of

___

___

___

What was the date of your loss?

___

___

___

Express the grief you feel in 10 words

___

___

___

List 10 things worth striving for

___

___

___

"I am still healing, and the journey of healing starts with me"

Today I am grieving the loss of

_____

_____

_____

What was the date of your loss?

_____

_____

_____

Express the grief you feel in 10 words

_____

_____

_____

List 10 things worth striving for

_____

_____

_____

"I am still healing, and the journey of healing starts with me"

Today I am grieving the loss of

_____

_____

_____

What was the date of your loss?

_____

_____

_____

Express the grief you feel in 10 words

_____

_____

_____

List 10 things worth striving for

_____

_____

_____

"I am still healing, and the journey of healing starts with me"

DAY 161

Today I am grieving the loss of

_____

_____

_____

What was the date of your loss?

_____

_____

_____

Express the grief you feel in 10 words

_____

_____

_____

List 10 things worth striving for

_____

_____

_____

"I am still healing, and the journey of healing starts with me"

DAY 162

Today I am grieving the loss of

_____

_____

_____

What was the date of your loss?

_____

_____

_____

Express the grief you feel in 10 words

_____

_____

_____

List 10 things worth striving for

_____

_____

_____

"I am still healing, and the journey of healing starts with me"

DAY 163

Today I am grieving the loss of

_____

_____

_____

What was the date of your loss?

_____

_____

_____

Express the grief you feel in 10 words

_____

_____

_____

List 10 things worth striving for

_____

_____

_____

"I am still healing, and the journey of healing starts with me"

Today I am grieving the loss of

_____

_____

_____

What was the date of your loss?

_____

_____

_____

Express the grief you feel in 10 words

_____

_____

_____

List 10 things worth striving for

_____

_____

_____

"I am still healing, and the journey of healing starts with me"

DAY 165

Today I am grieving the loss of

___

What was the date of your loss?

___

Express the grief you feel in 10 words

___

List 10 things worth striving for

___

"I am still healing, and the journey of healing starts with me"

DAY 166

Today I am grieving the loss of

_____

_____

_____

What was the date of your loss?

_____

_____

_____

Express the grief you feel in 10 words

_____

_____

_____

List 10 things worth striving for

_____

_____

_____

"I am still healing, and the journey of healing starts with me"

DAY 167

Today I am grieving the loss of

_____

_____

_____

What was the date of your loss?

_____

_____

_____

Express the grief you feel in 10 words

_____

_____

_____

List 10 things worth striving for

_____

_____

_____

"I am still healing, and the journey of healing starts with me"

Today I am grieving the loss of

_____

_____

_____

What was the date of your loss?

_____

_____

Express the grief you feel in 10 words

_____

_____

_____

List 10 things worth striving for

_____

_____

_____

"I am still healing, and the journey of healing starts with me"

DAY 169

Today I am grieving the loss of

_____

_____

_____

What was the date of your loss?

_____

_____

_____

Express the grief you feel in 10 words

_____

_____

_____

List 10 things worth striving for

_____

_____

_____

"I am still healing, and the journey of healing starts with me"

Today I am grieving the loss of

___

What was the date of your loss?

___

Express the grief you feel in 10 words

___

List 10 things worth striving for

___

"I am still healing, and the journey of healing starts with me"

DAY 171

Today I am grieving the loss of

_____
_____
_____

What was the date of your loss?

_____
_____
_____

Express the grief you feel in 10 words

_____
_____
_____

List 10 things worth striving for

_____
_____
_____

"I am still healing, and the journey of healing starts with me"

DAY 172

Today I am grieving the loss of

_____

_____

_____

What was the date of your loss?

_____

_____

_____

Express the grief you feel in 10 words

_____

_____

_____

List 10 things worth striving for

_____

_____

_____

"I am still healing, and the journey of healing starts with me"

DAY 173

Today I am grieving the loss of

_____

_____

_____

What was the date of your loss?

_____

_____

_____

Express the grief you feel in 10 words

_____

_____

_____

List 10 things worth striving for

_____

_____

_____

"I am still healing, and the journey of healing starts with me"

DAY 174

Today I am grieving the loss of

_____

_____

_____

What was the date of your loss?

_____

_____

_____

Express the grief you feel in 10 words

_____

_____

_____

List 10 things worth striving for

_____

_____

_____

"I am still healing, and the journey of healing starts with me"

DAY 175

Today I am grieving the loss of

___

What was the date of your loss?

___

Express the grief you feel in 10 words

___

List 10 things worth striving for

___

"I am still healing, and the journey of healing starts with me"

DAY 176

Today I am grieving the loss of

_____

_____

_____

What was the date of your loss?

_____

_____

_____

Express the grief you feel in 10 words

_____

_____

_____

List 10 things worth striving for

_____

_____

_____

"I am still healing, and the journey of healing starts with me"

DAY 177

Today I am grieving the loss of

_____

_____

_____

What was the date of your loss?

_____

_____

_____

Express the grief you feel in 10 words

_____

_____

_____

List 10 things worth striving for

_____

_____

_____

"I am still healing, and the journey of healing starts with me"

Today I am grieving the loss of

_____
_____
_____

What was the date of your loss?

_____
_____
_____

Express the grief you feel in 10 words

_____
_____
_____

List 10 things worth striving for

_____
_____
_____

"I am still healing, and the journey of healing starts with me"

DAY 179

Today I am grieving the loss of

_____

_____

_____

What was the date of your loss?

_____

_____

_____

Express the grief you feel in 10 words

_____

_____

_____

List 10 things worth striving for

_____

_____

_____

"I am still healing, and the journey of healing starts with me"

DAY 180

Today I am grieving the loss of

_____

_____

_____

What was the date of your loss?

_____

_____

_____

Express the grief you feel in 10 words

_____

_____

_____

List 10 things worth striving for

_____

_____

_____

"I am still healing, and the journey of healing starts with me"

Today I am grieving the loss of

_____

_____

_____

What was the date of your loss?

_____

_____

_____

Express the grief you feel in 10 words

_____

_____

_____

List 10 things worth striving for

_____

_____

_____

"I am still healing, and the journey of healing starts with me"

Today I am grieving the loss of

_____

_____

_____

What was the date of your loss?

_____

_____

_____

Express the grief you feel in 10 words

_____

_____

_____

List 10 things worth striving for

_____

_____

_____

"I am still healing, and the journey of healing starts with me"

DAY 183

Today I am grieving the loss of

_____

_____

_____

What was the date of your loss?

_____

_____

_____

Express the grief you feel in 10 words

_____

_____

_____

List 10 things worth striving for

_____

_____

_____

"I am still healing, and the journey of healing starts with me"

Today I am grieving the loss of

_____

_____

_____

What was the date of your loss?

_____

_____

_____

Express the grief you feel in 10 words

_____

_____

_____

List 10 things worth striving for

_____

_____

_____

"I am still healing, and the journey of healing starts with me"

DAY 185

Today I am grieving the loss of

_____

_____

_____

What was the date of your loss?

_____

_____

_____

Express the grief you feel in 10 words

_____

_____

_____

List 10 things worth striving for

_____

_____

_____

"I am still healing, and the journey of healing starts with me"

DAY 186

Today I am grieving the loss of

___

What was the date of your loss?

___

Express the grief you feel in 10 words

___

List 10 things worth striving for

___

"I am still healing, and the journey of healing starts with me"

DAY 187

Today I am grieving the loss of

___

What was the date of your loss?

___

Express the grief you feel in 10 words

___

List 10 things worth striving for

___

"I am still healing, and the journey of healing starts with me"

DAY 188

Today I am grieving the loss of

_____

_____

_____

What was the date of your loss?

_____

_____

_____

Express the grief you feel in 10 words

_____

_____

_____

List 10 things worth striving for

_____

_____

_____

"I am still healing, and the journey of healing starts with me"

DAY 189

Today I am grieving the loss of

_____

_____

_____

What was the date of your loss?

_____

_____

_____

Express the grief you feel in 10 words

_____

_____

_____

List 10 things worth striving for

_____

_____

_____

"I am still healing, and the journey of healing starts with me"

DAY 190

Today I am grieving the loss of

_____

_____

_____

What was the date of your loss?

_____

_____

_____

Express the grief you feel in 10 words

_____

_____

_____

List 10 things worth striving for

_____

_____

_____

"I am still healing, and the journey of healing starts with me"

DAY 191

Today I am grieving the loss of

_____

_____

_____

What was the date of your loss?

_____

_____

_____

Express the grief you feel in 10 words

_____

_____

_____

List 10 things worth striving for

_____

_____

_____

"I am still healing, and the journey of healing starts with me"

DAY 192

Today I am grieving the loss of

_____

_____

_____

What was the date of your loss?

_____

_____

_____

Express the grief you feel in 10 words

_____

_____

_____

List 10 things worth striving for

_____

_____

_____

"I am still healing, and the journey of healing starts with me"

DAY 193

Today I am grieving the loss of

_____

_____

_____

What was the date of your loss?

_____

_____

_____

Express the grief you feel in 10 words

_____

_____

_____

List 10 things worth striving for

_____

_____

_____

"I am still healing, and the journey of healing starts with me"

DAY 194

Today I am grieving the loss of

_____
_____
_____

What was the date of your loss?

_____
_____
_____

Express the grief you feel in 10 words

_____
_____
_____

List 10 things worth striving for

_____
_____
_____

"I am still healing, and the journey of healing starts with me"

DAY 195

Today I am grieving the loss of

_____

_____

_____

What was the date of your loss?

_____

_____

_____

Express the grief you feel in 10 words

_____

_____

_____

List 10 things worth striving for

_____

_____

_____

"I am still healing, and the journey of healing starts with me"

DAY 196

Today I am grieving the loss of

___

What was the date of your loss?

___

Express the grief you feel in 10 words

___

List 10 things worth striving for

___

"I am still healing, and the journey of healing starts with me"

DAY 197

Today I am grieving the loss of

___

What was the date of your loss?

___

Express the grief you feel in 10 words

___

List 10 things worth striving for

___

"I am still healing, and the journey of healing starts with me"

DAY 198

Today I am grieving the loss of

_____

_____

_____

What was the date of your loss?

_____

_____

_____

Express the grief you feel in 10 words

_____

_____

_____

List 10 things worth striving for

_____

_____

_____

"I am still healing, and the journey of healing starts with me"

DAY 199

Today I am grieving the loss of

_____

_____

_____

What was the date of your loss?

_____

_____

_____

Express the grief you feel in 10 words

_____

_____

_____

List 10 things worth striving for

_____

_____

_____

"I am still healing, and the journey of healing starts with me"

DAY 200

Today I am grieving the loss of

_____

_____

_____

What was the date of your loss?

_____

_____

_____

Express the grief you feel in 10 words

_____

_____

_____

List 10 things worth striving for

_____

_____

_____

"I am still healing, and the journey of healing starts with me"

DAY 201

Today I am grieving the loss of

_____

_____

_____

What was the date of your loss?

_____

_____

_____

Express the grief you feel in 10 words

_____

_____

_____

List 10 things worth striving for

_____

_____

_____

"I am still healing, and the journey of healing starts with me"

DAY 202

Today I am grieving the loss of

___

What was the date of your loss?

___

Express the grief you feel in 10 words

___

List 10 things worth striving for

___

"I am still healing, and the journey of healing starts with me"

DAY 203

Today I am grieving the loss of

___

What was the date of your loss?

___

Express the grief you feel in 10 words

___

List 10 things worth striving for

___

"I am still healing, and the journey of healing starts with me"

Today I am grieving the loss of

_____

_____

_____

What was the date of your loss?

_____

_____

_____

Express the grief you feel in 10 words

_____

_____

_____

List 10 things worth striving for

_____

_____

_____

"I am still healing, and the journey of healing starts with me"

DAY 205

Today I am grieving the loss of

___

What was the date of your loss?

___

Express the grief you feel in 10 words

___

List 10 things worth striving for

___

"I am still healing, and the journey of healing starts with me"

DAY 206

Today I am grieving the loss of

_____
_____
_____

What was the date of your loss?

_____
_____
_____

Express the grief you feel in 10 words

_____
_____
_____

List 10 things worth striving for

_____
_____
_____

"I am still healing, and the journey of healing starts with me"

DAY 207

Today I am grieving the loss of

___

What was the date of your loss?

___

Express the grief you feel in 10 words

___

List 10 things worth striving for

___

"I am still healing, and the journey of healing starts with me"

DAY 208

Today I am grieving the loss of

_____

_____

_____

What was the date of your loss?

_____

_____

_____

Express the grief you feel in 10 words

_____

_____

_____

List 10 things worth striving for

_____

_____

_____

"I am still healing, and the journey of healing starts with me"

DAY 209

Today I am grieving the loss of

_____

_____

_____

What was the date of your loss?

_____

_____

_____

Express the grief you feel in 10 words

_____

_____

_____

List 10 things worth striving for

_____

_____

_____

"I am still healing, and the journey of healing starts with me"

DAY 210

Today I am grieving the loss of

_____

_____

_____

What was the date of your loss?

_____

_____

_____

Express the grief you feel in 10 words

_____

_____

_____

List 10 things worth striving for

_____

_____

_____

"I am still healing, and the journey of healing starts with me"

DAY 211

Today I am grieving the loss of

___

What was the date of your loss?

___

Express the grief you feel in 10 words

___

List 10 things worth striving for

___

"I am still healing, and the journey of healing starts with me"

DAY 212

Today I am grieving the loss of

_____

_____

_____

What was the date of your loss?

_____

_____

_____

Express the grief you feel in 10 words

_____

_____

_____

List 10 things worth striving for

_____

_____

_____

"I am still healing, and the journey of healing starts with me"

DAY 213

Today I am grieving the loss of

_____

_____

_____

What was the date of your loss?

_____

_____

_____

Express the grief you feel in 10 words

_____

_____

_____

List 10 things worth striving for

_____

_____

_____

"I am still healing, and the journey of healing starts with me"

DAY 214

Today I am grieving the loss of

_____

_____

_____

What was the date of your loss?

_____

_____

_____

Express the grief you feel in 10 words

_____

_____

_____

List 10 things worth striving for

_____

_____

_____

"I am still healing, and the journey of healing starts with me"

DAY 215

Today I am grieving the loss of

___

What was the date of your loss?

___

Express the grief you feel in 10 words

___

List 10 things worth striving for

___

"I am still healing, and the journey of healing starts with me"

DAY 216

Today I am grieving the loss of

What was the date of your loss?

Express the grief you feel in 10 words

List 10 things worth striving for

"I am still healing, and the journey of healing starts with me"

DAY 217

Today I am grieving the loss of

_____
_____
_____

What was the date of your loss?

_____
_____
_____

Express the grief you feel in 10 words

_____
_____
_____

List 10 things worth striving for

_____
_____
_____

"I am still healing, and the journey of healing starts with me"

Today I am grieving the loss of

___

What was the date of your loss?

___

Express the grief you feel in 10 words

___

List 10 things worth striving for

___

"I am still healing, and the journey of healing starts with me"

DAY 219

Today I am grieving the loss of

___

What was the date of your loss?

___

Express the grief you feel in 10 words

___

List 10 things worth striving for

___

"I am still healing, and the journey of healing starts with me"

DAY 220

Today I am grieving the loss of

_____

_____

_____

What was the date of your loss?

_____

_____

_____

Express the grief you feel in 10 words

_____

_____

_____

List 10 things worth striving for

_____

_____

_____

"I am still healing, and the journey of healing starts with me"

DAY 221

Today I am grieving the loss of

_____

_____

_____

What was the date of your loss?

_____

_____

_____

Express the grief you feel in 10 words

_____

_____

_____

List 10 things worth striving for

_____

_____

_____

"I am still healing, and the journey of healing starts with me"

DAY 222

Today I am grieving the loss of

_____

_____

_____

What was the date of your loss?

_____

_____

_____

Express the grief you feel in 10 words

_____

_____

_____

List 10 things worth striving for

_____

_____

_____

"I am still healing, and the journey of healing starts with me"

DAY 223

Today I am grieving the loss of

_____

_____

_____

What was the date of your loss?

_____

_____

_____

Express the grief you feel in 10 words

_____

_____

_____

List 10 things worth striving for

_____

_____

_____

"I am still healing, and the journey of healing starts with me"

DAY 224

Today I am grieving the loss of

_____
_____
_____

What was the date of your loss?

_____
_____
_____

Express the grief you feel in 10 words

_____
_____
_____

List 10 things worth striving for

_____
_____
_____

"I am still healing, and the journey of healing starts with me"

Today I am grieving the loss of

_____

_____

_____

What was the date of your loss?

_____

_____

_____

Express the grief you feel in 10 words

_____

_____

_____

List 10 things worth striving for

_____

_____

_____

"I am still healing, and the journey of healing starts with me"

Today I am grieving the loss of

_____

_____

_____

What was the date of your loss?

_____

_____

_____

Express the grief you feel in 10 words

_____

_____

_____

List 10 things worth striving for

_____

_____

_____

"I am still healing, and the journey of healing starts with me"

Today I am grieving the loss of

_____

_____

_____

What was the date of your loss?

_____

_____

_____

Express the grief you feel in 10 words

_____

_____

_____

List 10 things worth striving for

_____

_____

_____

"I am still healing, and the journey of healing starts with me"

DAY 228

Today I am grieving the loss of

_____

_____

_____

What was the date of your loss?

_____

_____

_____

Express the grief you feel in 10 words

_____

_____

_____

List 10 things worth striving for

_____

_____

_____

"I am still healing, and the journey of healing starts with me"

DAY 229

Today I am grieving the loss of

___

___

What was the date of your loss?

___

___

Express the grief you feel in 10 words

___

___

List 10 things worth striving for

___

___

"I am still healing, and the journey of healing starts with me"

DAY 230

Today I am grieving the loss of

___
___
___

What was the date of your loss?

___
___
___

Express the grief you feel in 10 words

___
___
___

List 10 things worth striving for

___
___
___

"I am still healing, and the journey of healing starts with me"

DAY 231

Today I am grieving the loss of

_____

_____

_____

What was the date of your loss?

_____

_____

_____

Express the grief you feel in 10 words

_____

_____

_____

List 10 things worth striving for

_____

_____

_____

"I am still healing, and the journey of healing starts with me"

Today I am grieving the loss of

_____

_____

_____

What was the date of your loss?

_____

_____

_____

Express the grief you feel in 10 words

_____

_____

_____

List 10 things worth striving for

_____

_____

_____

"I am still healing, and the journey of healing starts with me"

Today I am grieving the loss of

_____

_____

_____

What was the date of your loss?

_____

_____

_____

Express the grief you feel in 10 words

_____

_____

_____

List 10 things worth striving for

_____

_____

_____

"I am still healing, and the journey of healing starts with me"

Today I am grieving the loss of

_____

_____

_____

What was the date of your loss?

_____

_____

_____

Express the grief you feel in 10 words

_____

_____

_____

List 10 things worth striving for

_____

_____

_____

"I am still healing, and the journey of healing starts with me"

Today I am grieving the loss of

_____

_____

_____

What was the date of your loss?

_____

_____

_____

Express the grief you feel in 10 words

_____

_____

_____

List 10 things worth striving for

_____

_____

_____

"I am still healing, and the journey of healing starts with me"

DAY 236

Today I am grieving the loss of

_____

_____

_____

What was the date of your loss?

_____

_____

_____

Express the grief you feel in 10 words

_____

_____

_____

List 10 things worth striving for

_____

_____

_____

"I am still healing, and the journey of healing starts with me"

Today I am grieving the loss of

_____

_____

_____

What was the date of your loss?

_____

_____

_____

Express the grief you feel in 10 words

_____

_____

_____

List 10 things worth striving for

_____

_____

_____

"I am still healing, and the journey of healing starts with me"

DAY 238

Today I am grieving the loss of

_____

_____

_____

What was the date of your loss?

_____

_____

_____

Express the grief you feel in 10 words

_____

_____

_____

List 10 things worth striving for

_____

_____

_____

"I am still healing, and the journey of healing starts with me"

Today I am grieving the loss of

_____

_____

_____

What was the date of your loss?

_____

_____

_____

Express the grief you feel in 10 words

_____

_____

_____

List 10 things worth striving for

_____

_____

_____

"I am still healing, and the journey of healing starts with me"

DAY 240

Today I am grieving the loss of

_____

_____

_____

What was the date of your loss?

_____

_____

_____

Express the grief you feel in 10 words

_____

_____

_____

List 10 things worth striving for

_____

_____

_____

"I am still healing, and the journey of healing starts with me"

DAY 241

Today I am grieving the loss of

_____

_____

_____

What was the date of your loss?

_____

_____

_____

Express the grief you feel in 10 words

_____

_____

_____

List 10 things worth striving for

_____

_____

_____

"I am still healing, and the journey of healing starts with me"

DAY 242

Today I am grieving the loss of

_____

_____

_____

What was the date of your loss?

_____

_____

_____

Express the grief you feel in 10 words

_____

_____

_____

List 10 things worth striving for

_____

_____

_____

"I am still healing, and the journey of healing starts with me"

Today I am grieving the loss of

_____

_____

_____

What was the date of your loss?

_____

_____

_____

Express the grief you feel in 10 words

_____

_____

_____

List 10 things worth striving for

_____

_____

_____

"I am still healing, and the journey of healing starts with me"

DAY 244

Today I am grieving the loss of

_____

_____

_____

What was the date of your loss?

_____

_____

_____

Express the grief you feel in 10 words

_____

_____

_____

List 10 things worth striving for

_____

_____

_____

"I am still healing, and the journey of healing starts with me"

DAY 245

Today I am grieving the loss of

_____

_____

_____

What was the date of your loss?

_____

_____

_____

Express the grief you feel in 10 words

_____

_____

_____

List 10 things worth striving for

_____

_____

_____

"I am still healing, and the journey of healing starts with me"

Today I am grieving the loss of

_____

_____

_____

What was the date of your loss?

_____

_____

_____

Express the grief you feel in 10 words

_____

_____

_____

List 10 things worth striving for

_____

_____

_____

"I am still healing, and the journey of healing starts with me"

Today I am grieving the loss of

_____

_____

_____

What was the date of your loss?

_____

_____

_____

Express the grief you feel in 10 words

_____

_____

_____

List 10 things worth striving for

_____

_____

_____

"I am still healing, and the journey of healing starts with me"

Today I am grieving the loss of

___

What was the date of your loss?

___

Express the grief you feel in 10 words

___

List 10 things worth striving for

___

"I am still healing, and the journey of healing starts with me"

DAY 249

Today I am grieving the loss of

___

What was the date of your loss?

___

Express the grief you feel in 10 words

___

List 10 things worth striving for

___

"I am still healing, and the journey of healing starts with me"

DAY 250

Today I am grieving the loss of

_____

_____

_____

What was the date of your loss?

_____

_____

_____

Express the grief you feel in 10 words

_____

_____

_____

List 10 things worth striving for

_____

_____

_____

"I am still healing, and the journey of healing starts with me"

DAY 251

Today I am grieving the loss of

___

What was the date of your loss?

___

Express the grief you feel in 10 words

___

List 10 things worth striving for

___

"I am still healing, and the journey of healing starts with me"

DAY 252

Today I am grieving the loss of

_____

_____

_____

What was the date of your loss?

_____

_____

_____

Express the grief you feel in 10 words

_____

_____

_____

List 10 things worth striving for

_____

_____

_____

"I am still healing, and the journey of healing starts with me"

DAY 253

Today I am grieving the loss of

_____

_____

_____

What was the date of your loss?

_____

_____

_____

Express the grief you feel in 10 words

_____

_____

_____

List 10 things worth striving for

_____

_____

_____

"I am still healing, and the journey of healing starts with me"

DAY 254

Today I am grieving the loss of

___
___
___

What was the date of your loss?

___
___
___

Express the grief you feel in 10 words

___
___
___

List 10 things worth striving for

___
___
___

"I am still healing, and the journey of healing starts with me"

DAY 255

Today I am grieving the loss of

___

What was the date of your loss?

___

Express the grief you feel in 10 words

___

List 10 things worth striving for

___

"I am still healing, and the journey of healing starts with me"

DAY 256

Today I am grieving the loss of

_____

_____

_____

What was the date of your loss?

_____

_____

_____

Express the grief you feel in 10 words

_____

_____

_____

List 10 things worth striving for

_____

_____

_____

"I am still healing, and the journey of healing starts with me"

DAY 257

Today I am grieving the loss of

_____

_____

_____

What was the date of your loss?

_____

_____

_____

Express the grief you feel in 10 words

_____

_____

_____

List 10 things worth striving for

_____

_____

_____

"I am still healing, and the journey of healing starts with me"

DAY 258

Today I am grieving the loss of

_____

_____

_____

What was the date of your loss?

_____

_____

_____

Express the grief you feel in 10 words

_____

_____

_____

List 10 things worth striving for

_____

_____

_____

"I am still healing, and the journey of healing starts with me"

Today I am grieving the loss of

_____

_____

_____

What was the date of your loss?

_____

_____

_____

Express the grief you feel in 10 words

_____

_____

_____

List 10 things worth striving for

_____

_____

_____

"I am still healing, and the journey of healing starts with me"

DAY 260

Today I am grieving the loss of

_____

_____

_____

What was the date of your loss?

_____

_____

_____

Express the grief you feel in 10 words

_____

_____

_____

List 10 things worth striving for

_____

_____

_____

"I am still healing, and the journey of healing starts with me"

DAY 261

Today I am grieving the loss of

_____
_____
_____

What was the date of your loss?

_____
_____
_____

Express the grief you feel in 10 words

_____
_____
_____

List 10 things worth striving for

_____
_____
_____

"I am still healing, and the journey of healing starts with me"

Today I am grieving the loss of

___

What was the date of your loss?

___

Express the grief you feel in 10 words

___

List 10 things worth striving for

___

"I am still healing, and the journey of healing starts with me"

DAY 263

Today I am grieving the loss of

___

What was the date of your loss?

___

Express the grief you feel in 10 words

___

List 10 things worth striving for

___

"I am still healing, and the journey of healing starts with me"

Today I am grieving the loss of

_____

_____

_____

What was the date of your loss?

_____

_____

_____

Express the grief you feel in 10 words

_____

_____

_____

List 10 things worth striving for

_____

_____

_____

"I am still healing, and the journey of healing starts with me"

Today I am grieving the loss of

_____
_____
_____

What was the date of your loss?

_____
_____
_____

Express the grief you feel in 10 words

_____
_____
_____

List 10 things worth striving for

_____
_____
_____

"I am still healing, and the journey of healing starts with me"

Today I am grieving the loss of

_____

_____

_____

What was the date of your loss?

_____

_____

_____

Express the grief you feel in 10 words

_____

_____

_____

List 10 things worth striving for

_____

_____

_____

"I am still healing, and the journey of healing starts with me"

DAY 267

Today I am grieving the loss of

_____

_____

_____

What was the date of your loss?

_____

_____

_____

Express the grief you feel in 10 words

_____

_____

_____

List 10 things worth striving for

_____

_____

_____

"I am still healing, and the journey of healing starts with me"

DAY 268

Today I am grieving the loss of

_____

_____

_____

What was the date of your loss?

_____

_____

_____

Express the grief you feel in 10 words

_____

_____

_____

List 10 things worth striving for

_____

_____

_____

"I am still healing, and the journey of healing starts with me"

Today I am grieving the loss of

_____

_____

_____

What was the date of your loss?

_____

_____

_____

Express the grief you feel in 10 words

_____

_____

_____

List 10 things worth striving for

_____

_____

_____

"I am still healing, and the journey of healing starts with me"

DAY 270

Today I am grieving the loss of

_____

_____

_____

What was the date of your loss?

_____

_____

_____

Express the grief you feel in 10 words

_____

_____

_____

List 10 things worth striving for

_____

_____

_____

"I am still healing, and the journey of healing starts with me"

DAY 271

Today I am grieving the loss of

_____

_____

_____

What was the date of your loss?

_____

_____

_____

Express the grief you feel in 10 words

_____

_____

_____

List 10 things worth striving for

_____

_____

_____

"I am still healing, and the journey of healing starts with me"

DAY 272

Today I am grieving the loss of

_____

_____

_____

What was the date of your loss?

_____

_____

_____

Express the grief you feel in 10 words

_____

_____

_____

List 10 things worth striving for

_____

_____

_____

"I am still healing, and the journey of healing starts with me"

Today I am grieving the loss of

_____

_____

_____

What was the date of your loss?

_____

_____

_____

Express the grief you feel in 10 words

_____

_____

_____

List 10 things worth striving for

_____

_____

_____

"I am still healing, and the journey of healing starts with me"

Today I am grieving the loss of

___

What was the date of your loss?

___

Express the grief you feel in 10 words

___

List 10 things worth striving for

___

"I am still healing, and the journey of healing starts with me"

DAY 275

Today I am grieving the loss of

_____

_____

_____

What was the date of your loss?

_____

_____

_____

Express the grief you feel in 10 words

_____

_____

_____

List 10 things worth striving for

_____

_____

_____

"I am still healing, and the journey of healing starts with me"

Today I am grieving the loss of

_____

_____

_____

What was the date of your loss?

_____

_____

_____

Express the grief you feel in 10 words

_____

_____

_____

List 10 things worth striving for

_____

_____

_____

"I am still healing, and the journey of healing starts with me"

DAY 277

Today I am grieving the loss of

What was the date of your loss?

Express the grief you feel in 10 words

List 10 things worth striving for

"I am still healing, and the journey of healing starts with me"

Today I am grieving the loss of

_____

_____

_____

What was the date of your loss?

_____

_____

_____

Express the grief you feel in 10 words

_____

_____

_____

List 10 things worth striving for

_____

_____

_____

"I am still healing, and the journey of healing starts with me"

Today I am grieving the loss of

_____

_____

_____

What was the date of your loss?

_____

_____

_____

Express the grief you feel in 10 words

_____

_____

_____

List 10 things worth striving for

_____

_____

_____

"I am still healing, and the journey of healing starts with me"

DAY 280

Today I am grieving the loss of

What was the date of your loss?

Express the grief you feel in 10 words

List 10 things worth striving for

"I am still healing, and the journey of healing starts with me"

Today I am grieving the loss of

_____

_____

_____

What was the date of your loss?

_____

_____

_____

Express the grief you feel in 10 words

_____

_____

_____

List 10 things worth striving for

_____

_____

_____

"I am still healing, and the journey of healing starts with me"

Today I am grieving the loss of

_____

_____

_____

What was the date of your loss?

_____

_____

_____

Express the grief you feel in 10 words

_____

_____

_____

List 10 things worth striving for

_____

_____

_____

"I am still healing, and the journey of healing starts with me"

Today I am grieving the loss of

_____

_____

_____

What was the date of your loss?

_____

_____

_____

Express the grief you feel in 10 words

_____

_____

_____

List 10 things worth striving for

_____

_____

_____

"I am still healing, and the journey of healing starts with me"

Today I am grieving the loss of

_____

_____

_____

What was the date of your loss?

_____

_____

_____

Express the grief you feel in 10 words

_____

_____

_____

List 10 things worth striving for

_____

_____

_____

"I am still healing, and the journey of healing starts with me"

Today I am grieving the loss of

_____

_____

_____

What was the date of your loss?

_____

_____

_____

Express the grief you feel in 10 words

_____

_____

_____

List 10 things worth striving for

_____

_____

_____

"I am still healing, and the journey of healing starts with me"

Today I am grieving the loss of

_____

_____

_____

What was the date of your loss?

_____

_____

_____

Express the grief you feel in 10 words

_____

_____

_____

List 10 things worth striving for

_____

_____

_____

"I am still healing, and the journey of healing starts with me"

DAY 287

Today I am grieving the loss of

_____
_____
_____

What was the date of your loss?

_____
_____
_____

Express the grief you feel in 10 words

_____
_____
_____

List 10 things worth striving for

_____
_____
_____

"I am still healing, and the journey of healing starts with me"

DAY 288

Today I am grieving the loss of

___

What was the date of your loss?

___

Express the grief you feel in 10 words

___

List 10 things worth striving for

___

"I am still healing, and the journey of healing starts with me"

DAY 289

Today I am grieving the loss of

_____

_____

_____

What was the date of your loss?

_____

_____

_____

Express the grief you feel in 10 words

_____

_____

_____

List 10 things worth striving for

_____

_____

_____

"I am still healing, and the journey of healing starts with me"

DAY 290

Today I am grieving the loss of

What was the date of your loss?

Express the grief you feel in 10 words

List 10 things worth striving for

"I am still healing, and the journey of healing starts with me"

DAY 291

Today I am grieving the loss of

_____
_____
_____

What was the date of your loss?

_____
_____
_____

Express the grief you feel in 10 words

_____
_____
_____

List 10 things worth striving for

_____
_____
_____

"I am still healing, and the journey of healing starts with me"

DAY 292

Today I am grieving the loss of

_____

_____

_____

What was the date of your loss?

_____

_____

_____

Express the grief you feel in 10 words

_____

_____

_____

List 10 things worth striving for

_____

_____

_____

"I am still healing, and the journey of healing starts with me"

DAY 293

Today I am grieving the loss of

_____

_____

_____

What was the date of your loss?

_____

_____

_____

Express the grief you feel in 10 words

_____

_____

_____

List 10 things worth striving for

_____

_____

_____

"I am still healing, and the journey of healing starts with me"

DAY 294

Today I am grieving the loss of

_____

_____

_____

What was the date of your loss?

_____

_____

_____

Express the grief you feel in 10 words

_____

_____

_____

List 10 things worth striving for

_____

_____

_____

"I am still healing, and the journey of healing starts with me"

Today I am grieving the loss of

_____

_____

_____

What was the date of your loss?

_____

_____

_____

Express the grief you feel in 10 words

_____

_____

_____

List 10 things worth striving for

_____

_____

_____

"I am still healing, and the journey of healing starts with me"

Today I am grieving the loss of

_____

_____

_____

What was the date of your loss?

_____

_____

_____

Express the grief you feel in 10 words

_____

_____

_____

List 10 things worth striving for

_____

_____

_____

"I am still healing, and the journey of healing starts with me"

DAY 297

Today I am grieving the loss of

_____

_____

_____

What was the date of your loss?

_____

_____

_____

Express the grief you feel in 10 words

_____

_____

_____

List 10 things worth striving for

_____

_____

_____

"I am still healing, and the journey of healing starts with me"

Today I am grieving the loss of

___

What was the date of your loss?

___

Express the grief you feel in 10 words

___

List 10 things worth striving for

___

"I am still healing, and the journey of healing starts with me"

DAY 299

Today I am grieving the loss of

_____

_____

_____

What was the date of your loss?

_____

_____

_____

Express the grief you feel in 10 words

_____

_____

_____

List 10 things worth striving for

_____

_____

_____

"I am still healing, and the journey of healing starts with me"

DAY 300

Today I am grieving the loss of

___

What was the date of your loss?

___

Express the grief you feel in 10 words

___

List 10 things worth striving for

___

"I am still healing, and the journey of healing starts with me"

DAY 301

Today I am grieving the loss of

___

What was the date of your loss?

___

Express the grief you feel in 10 words

___

List 10 things worth striving for

___

"I am still healing, and the journey of healing starts with me"

DAY 302

Today I am grieving the loss of

_____

_____

_____

What was the date of your loss?

_____

_____

_____

Express the grief you feel in 10 words

_____

_____

_____

List 10 things worth striving for

_____

_____

_____

"I am still healing, and the journey of healing starts with me"

Today I am grieving the loss of

_____

_____

_____

What was the date of your loss?

_____

_____

_____

Express the grief you feel in 10 words

_____

_____

_____

List 10 things worth striving for

_____

_____

_____

"I am still healing, and the journey of healing starts with me"

Today I am grieving the loss of

_____

_____

_____

What was the date of your loss?

_____

_____

_____

Express the grief you feel in 10 words

_____

_____

_____

List 10 things worth striving for

_____

_____

_____

"I am still healing, and the journey of healing starts with me"

Today I am grieving the loss of

_____

_____

_____

What was the date of your loss?

_____

_____

_____

Express the grief you feel in 10 words

_____

_____

_____

List 10 things worth striving for

_____

_____

_____

"I am still healing, and the journey of healing starts with me"

DAY 306

Today I am grieving the loss of

_____

_____

_____

What was the date of your loss?

_____

_____

_____

Express the grief you feel in 10 words

_____

_____

_____

List 10 things worth striving for

_____

_____

_____

"I am still healing, and the journey of healing starts with me"

Today I am grieving the loss of

___

What was the date of your loss?

___

Express the grief you feel in 10 words

___

List 10 things worth striving for

___

"I am still healing, and the journey of healing starts with me"

DAY 308

Today I am grieving the loss of

_____
_____
_____

What was the date of your loss?

_____
_____
_____

Express the grief you feel in 10 words

_____
_____
_____

List 10 things worth striving for

_____
_____
_____

"I am still healing, and the journey of healing starts with me"

Today I am grieving the loss of

_____

_____

_____

What was the date of your loss?

_____

_____

_____

Express the grief you feel in 10 words

_____

_____

_____

List 10 things worth striving for

_____

_____

_____

"I am still healing, and the journey of healing starts with me"

DAY 310

Today I am grieving the loss of

___

___

___

What was the date of your loss?

___

___

___

Express the grief you feel in 10 words

___

___

___

List 10 things worth striving for

___

___

___

"I am still healing, and the journey of healing starts with me"

Today I am grieving the loss of

_____

_____

_____

What was the date of your loss?

_____

_____

_____

Express the grief you feel in 10 words

_____

_____

_____

List 10 things worth striving for

_____

_____

_____

"I am still healing, and the journey of healing starts with me"

DAY 312

Today I am grieving the loss of

_____
_____
_____

What was the date of your loss?

_____
_____
_____

Express the grief you feel in 10 words

_____
_____
_____

List 10 things worth striving for

_____
_____
_____

"I am still healing, and the journey of healing starts with me"

DAY 313

Today I am grieving the loss of

___

What was the date of your loss?

___

Express the grief you feel in 10 words

___

List 10 things worth striving for

___

"I am still healing, and the journey of healing starts with me"

DAY 314

Today I am grieving the loss of

_____

_____

_____

What was the date of your loss?

_____

_____

_____

Express the grief you feel in 10 words

_____

_____

_____

List 10 things worth striving for

_____

_____

_____

"I am still healing, and the journey of healing starts with me"

DAY 315

Today I am grieving the loss of

_____

_____

_____

What was the date of your loss?

_____

_____

_____

Express the grief you feel in 10 words

_____

_____

_____

List 10 things worth striving for

_____

_____

_____

"I am still healing, and the journey of healing starts with me"

Today I am grieving the loss of

What was the date of your loss?

Express the grief you feel in 10 words

List 10 things worth striving for

"I am still healing, and the journey of healing starts with me"

Today I am grieving the loss of

_____

_____

_____

What was the date of your loss?

_____

_____

_____

Express the grief you feel in 10 words

_____

_____

_____

List 10 things worth striving for

_____

_____

_____

"I am still healing, and the journey of healing starts with me"

Today I am grieving the loss of

_____

_____

_____

What was the date of your loss?

_____

_____

Express the grief you feel in 10 words

_____

_____

_____

List 10 things worth striving for

_____

_____

_____

"I am still healing, and the journey of healing starts with me"

Today I am grieving the loss of

_____

_____

_____

What was the date of your loss?

_____

_____

_____

Express the grief you feel in 10 words

_____

_____

_____

List 10 things worth striving for

_____

_____

_____

"I am still healing, and the journey of healing starts with me"

Today I am grieving the loss of

_____

_____

_____

What was the date of your loss?

_____

_____

_____

Express the grief you feel in 10 words

_____

_____

_____

List 10 things worth striving for

_____

_____

_____

"I am still healing, and the journey of healing starts with me"

Today I am grieving the loss of

_____

_____

_____

What was the date of your loss?

_____

_____

_____

Express the grief you feel in 10 words

_____

_____

_____

List 10 things worth striving for

_____

_____

_____

"I am still healing, and the journey of healing starts with me"

DAY 322

Today I am grieving the loss of

_____
_____
_____

What was the date of your loss?

_____
_____
_____

Express the grief you feel in 10 words

_____
_____
_____

List 10 things worth striving for

_____
_____
_____

"I am still healing, and the journey of healing starts with me"

DAY 323

Today I am grieving the loss of

___

What was the date of your loss?

___

Express the grief you feel in 10 words

___

List 10 things worth striving for

___

"I am still healing, and the journey of healing starts with me"

DAY 324

Today I am grieving the loss of

_____

_____

_____

What was the date of your loss?

_____

_____

_____

Express the grief you feel in 10 words

_____

_____

_____

List 10 things worth striving for

_____

_____

_____

"I am still healing, and the journey of healing starts with me"

DAY 325

Today I am grieving the loss of

_____

_____

_____

What was the date of your loss?

_____

_____

_____

Express the grief you feel in 10 words

_____

_____

_____

List 10 things worth striving for

_____

_____

_____

"I am still healing, and the journey of healing starts with me"

DAY 326

Today I am grieving the loss of

_____

_____

_____

What was the date of your loss?

_____

_____

_____

Express the grief you feel in 10 words

_____

_____

_____

List 10 things worth striving for

_____

_____

_____

"I am still healing, and the journey of healing starts with me"

DAY 327

Today I am grieving the loss of

_____

_____

_____

What was the date of your loss?

_____

_____

_____

Express the grief you feel in 10 words

_____

_____

_____

List 10 things worth striving for

_____

_____

_____

"I am still healing, and the journey of healing starts with me"

DAY 328

Today I am grieving the loss of

_____

_____

_____

What was the date of your loss?

_____

_____

_____

Express the grief you feel in 10 words

_____

_____

_____

List 10 things worth striving for

_____

_____

_____

"I am still healing, and the journey of healing starts with me"

Today I am grieving the loss of

_____

_____

_____

What was the date of your loss?

_____

_____

_____

Express the grief you feel in 10 words

_____

_____

_____

List 10 things worth striving for

_____

_____

_____

"I am still healing, and the journey of healing starts with me"

Today I am grieving the loss of

_____

_____

_____

What was the date of your loss?

_____

_____

_____

Express the grief you feel in 10 words

_____

_____

_____

List 10 things worth striving for

_____

_____

_____

"I am still healing, and the journey of healing starts with me"

DAY 331

Today I am grieving the loss of

___

What was the date of your loss?

___

Express the grief you feel in 10 words

___

List 10 things worth striving for

___

"I am still healing, and the journey of healing starts with me"

DAY 332

Today I am grieving the loss of

_____

_____

_____

What was the date of your loss?

_____

_____

_____

Express the grief you feel in 10 words

_____

_____

_____

List 10 things worth striving for

_____

_____

_____

"I am still healing, and the journey of healing starts with me"

DAY 333

Today I am grieving the loss of

_____

_____

_____

What was the date of your loss?

_____

_____

_____

Express the grief you feel in 10 words

_____

_____

_____

List 10 things worth striving for

_____

_____

_____

"I am still healing, and the journey of healing starts with me"

DAY 334

Today I am grieving the loss of

_____

_____

_____

What was the date of your loss?

_____

_____

_____

Express the grief you feel in 10 words

_____

_____

_____

List 10 things worth striving for

_____

_____

_____

"I am still healing, and the journey of healing starts with me"

DAY 335

Today I am grieving the loss of

_____

_____

_____

What was the date of your loss?

_____

_____

_____

Express the grief you feel in 10 words

_____

_____

_____

List 10 things worth striving for

_____

_____

_____

"I am still healing, and the journey of healing starts with me"

DAY 336

Today I am grieving the loss of

_____

_____

_____

What was the date of your loss?

_____

_____

_____

Express the grief you feel in 10 words

_____

_____

_____

List 10 things worth striving for

_____

_____

_____

"I am still healing, and the journey of healing starts with me"

DAY 337

Today I am grieving the loss of

___

___

What was the date of your loss?

___

___

Express the grief you feel in 10 words

___

___

List 10 things worth striving for

___

___

"I am still healing, and the journey of healing starts with me"

Today I am grieving the loss of

_____

_____

_____

What was the date of your loss?

_____

_____

_____

Express the grief you feel in 10 words

_____

_____

_____

List 10 things worth striving for

_____

_____

_____

"I am still healing, and the journey of healing starts with me"

Today I am grieving the loss of

_____

_____

_____

What was the date of your loss?

_____

_____

_____

Express the grief you feel in 10 words

_____

_____

_____

List 10 things worth striving for

_____

_____

_____

"I am still healing, and the journey of healing starts with me"

Today I am grieving the loss of

_____

_____

_____

What was the date of your loss?

_____

_____

_____

Express the grief you feel in 10 words

_____

_____

_____

List 10 things worth striving for

_____

_____

_____

"I am still healing, and the journey of healing starts with me"

Today I am grieving the loss of

_____

_____

_____

What was the date of your loss?

_____

_____

_____

Express the grief you feel in 10 words

_____

_____

_____

List 10 things worth striving for

_____

_____

_____

"I am still healing, and the journey of healing starts with me"

DAY 342

Today I am grieving the loss of

_____

_____

_____

What was the date of your loss?

_____

_____

_____

Express the grief you feel in 10 words

_____

_____

_____

List 10 things worth striving for

_____

_____

_____

"I am still healing, and the journey of healing starts with me"

Today I am grieving the loss of

_____

_____

_____

What was the date of your loss?

_____

_____

_____

Express the grief you feel in 10 words

_____

_____

_____

List 10 things worth striving for

_____

_____

_____

"I am still healing, and the journey of healing starts with me"

DAY 344

Today I am grieving the loss of

_____

_____

_____

What was the date of your loss?

_____

_____

_____

Express the grief you feel in 10 words

_____

_____

_____

List 10 things worth striving for

_____

_____

_____

"I am still healing, and the journey of healing starts with me"

DAY 345

Today I am grieving the loss of

_____

_____

_____

What was the date of your loss?

_____

_____

_____

Express the grief you feel in 10 words

_____

_____

_____

List 10 things worth striving for

_____

_____

_____

"I am still healing, and the journey of healing starts with me"

DAY 346

Today I am grieving the loss of

_____
_____
_____

What was the date of your loss?

_____
_____
_____

Express the grief you feel in 10 words

_____
_____
_____

List 10 things worth striving for

_____
_____
_____

"I am still healing, and the journey of healing starts with me"

Today I am grieving the loss of

_____
_____
_____

What was the date of your loss?

_____
_____
_____

Express the grief you feel in 10 words

_____
_____
_____

List 10 things worth striving for

_____
_____
_____

"I am still healing, and the journey of healing starts with me"

Today I am grieving the loss of

_____

_____

_____

What was the date of your loss?

_____

_____

_____

Express the grief you feel in 10 words

_____

_____

_____

List 10 things worth striving for

_____

_____

_____

"I am still healing, and the journey of healing starts with me"

Today I am grieving the loss of

_____

_____

_____

What was the date of your loss?

_____

_____

_____

Express the grief you feel in 10 words

_____

_____

_____

List 10 things worth striving for

_____

_____

_____

"I am still healing, and the journey of healing starts with me"

Today I am grieving the loss of

_____

_____

_____

What was the date of your loss?

_____

_____

_____

Express the grief you feel in 10 words

_____

_____

_____

List 10 things worth striving for

_____

_____

_____

"I am still healing, and the journey of healing starts with me"

DAY 351

Today I am grieving the loss of

_____

_____

_____

What was the date of your loss?

_____

_____

_____

Express the grief you feel in 10 words

_____

_____

_____

List 10 things worth striving for

_____

_____

_____

"I am still healing, and the journey of healing starts with me"

DAY 352

Today I am grieving the loss of

What was the date of your loss?

Express the grief you feel in 10 words

List 10 things worth striving for

"I am still healing, and the journey of healing starts with me"

Today I am grieving the loss of

___

What was the date of your loss?

___

Express the grief you feel in 10 words

___

List 10 things worth striving for

___

"I am still healing, and the journey of healing starts with me"

Today I am grieving the loss of

_____
_____
_____

What was the date of your loss?

_____
_____
_____

Express the grief you feel in 10 words

_____
_____
_____

List 10 things worth striving for

_____
_____
_____

"I am still healing, and the journey of healing starts with me"

DAY 355

Today I am grieving the loss of

_____

_____

_____

What was the date of your loss?

_____

_____

_____

Express the grief you feel in 10 words

_____

_____

_____

List 10 things worth striving for

_____

_____

_____

"I am still healing, and the journey of healing starts with me"

DAY 356

Today I am grieving the loss of

_____

_____

_____

What was the date of your loss?

_____

_____

_____

Express the grief you feel in 10 words

_____

_____

_____

List 10 things worth striving for

_____

_____

_____

"I am still healing, and the journey of healing starts with me"

DAY 357

Today I am grieving the loss of

_____

_____

_____

What was the date of your loss?

_____

_____

_____

Express the grief you feel in 10 words

_____

_____

_____

List 10 things worth striving for

_____

_____

_____

"I am still healing, and the journey of healing starts with me"

DAY 358

Today I am grieving the loss of

_____

_____

_____

What was the date of your loss?

_____

_____

_____

Express the grief you feel in 10 words

_____

_____

_____

List 10 things worth striving for

_____

_____

_____

"I am still healing, and the journey of healing starts with me"

Today I am grieving the loss of

_____

_____

_____

What was the date of your loss?

_____

_____

_____

Express the grief you feel in 10 words

_____

_____

_____

List 10 things worth striving for

_____

_____

_____

"I am still healing, and the journey of healing starts with me"

DAY 360

Today I am grieving the loss of

_____
_____
_____

What was the date of your loss?

_____
_____
_____

Express the grief you feel in 10 words

_____
_____
_____

List 10 things worth striving for

_____
_____
_____

"I am still healing, and the journey of healing starts with me"

DAY 361

Today I am grieving the loss of

_____

_____

_____

What was the date of your loss?

_____

_____

_____

Express the grief you feel in 10 words

_____

_____

_____

List 10 things worth striving for

_____

_____

_____

"I am still healing, and the journey of healing starts with me"

DAY 362

Today I am grieving the loss of

_____
_____
_____

What was the date of your loss?

_____
_____
_____

Express the grief you feel in 10 words

_____
_____
_____

List 10 things worth striving for

_____
_____
_____

"I am still healing, and the journey of healing starts with me"

DAY 363

Today I am grieving the loss of

_____

_____

_____

What was the date of your loss?

_____

_____

_____

Express the grief you feel in 10 words

_____

_____

_____

List 10 things worth striving for

_____

_____

_____

"I am still healing, and the journey of healing starts with me"

DAY 364

Today I am grieving the loss of

_____

_____

_____

What was the date of your loss?

_____

_____

_____

Express the grief you feel in 10 words

_____

_____

_____

List 10 things worth striving for

_____

_____

_____

"I am still healing, and the journey of healing starts with me"

DAY 365

www.ingramcontent.com/pod-product-compliance
Lightning Source LLC
Chambersburg PA
CBHW041232240426
43673CB00010B/316